The Outpost at 3pm

GRAHAM FORD

The Outpost at 3pm

Copyright © 2020 by Graham Ford.

Paperback ISBN: 978-1-952982-45-3
Ebook ISBN: 978-1-952982-46-0

All rights reserved. No part in this book may be produced and transmitted in any form or by any means, electronic, or mechanical, including photocopying, recording, or by any information storage and retrieval system, without permission in writing from the copyright owner.

The views expressed in this work are solely those of the author and do not necessarily reflect the views of the publisher hereby disclaims any responsibility for them.

Published by Golden Ink Media Services   11/05/2020

Golden Ink Media Services
(302) 703-7235
support@goldeninkmediaservices@gmail.com

Acknowledgements

Some of these poems have been published
In the Mozzie magazine of Australia

Also by Graham Ford:

For Three Sins or Four
It's Confidential
True Hero Worship
Eternity in the Mirror

I would like to thank John Drake
For his invaluable input

In after days when grasses high
O'er top the stone where I shall lie
Though ill or well the world adjust
My slender claim to honoured dust
I shall not question or reply

Henry Austin Dobson

A Perfect Life (A Home)

Keen and cheerful
And secure in an expressive abode,
Our diligent children grew
In a devout and disciplined house
Organized so that each child
Can feel comfortable at home.

Coming upon our happy fare
As a river ran dry
Under the towering, sturdy gums,
God dozed as one at rest.
Luckily our house was blessed
Never to make Him angry.

Short, fat and out of shape,
I was a dopey catch
With feet as big as dinner plates.
Sooner than stand still
They would trip over on a whim
To gather dust like a door mat.

But my perfectly good wife
Would not leave me there.
I was not to forget my chores.
With a cry she was quick to apply
The urge to chase away my fears
Then work me without a wail.

A roving, lustful eye
Is for one who wants to die
With a gesture from his wife
At the hands of his priest

But, humbly, I was content
To live the life of a married man.

No suspicious adultery,
No straying from the path,
I lived the perfect life
With my wife; I toed the line.
I was no malcontent
Who invited the devil's disarray.

Affection was the category
Our sublime generosity fell into.
We danced in the evening.
We had a daily routine.
She was free to come and go,
To follow the dreams of her own.

In the town where we live.
There is a petulant river:
One that sulks in a winter trickle
Then flexes its muscles in a summer flood
As the rain pours down and marks its course
Along the banks of its ancient force.

On an arid Sunday I came
To say my fervent prayers:
To speak with the Almighty God,
To thank the gentle Lord Jesus
For the busy week gone by,
To ask God for more of the same.

Our many children flourish
In a blissful, bush setting
With God in their caring hearts.
Speaking happily of His wisdom
They make their youthful stand
But a few soon leave for the citadel's streets.

Together we age comfortably,
Certain of companionship.
To make the hours special:
She with her books and cups of tea,
I with my pen jotting of an idyll,
That was a nod to the presence of the Lord.

The Southern Cross

The awesome stars break out
On a cold, wintry night.
They have a full, wholesome glare.
The exciting Milky Way is up there,
A wonder to my ecstatic mind.

There is no other light in the sky
Except for the soft, feeble glow
Of a distant, active town -
A faraway burst of luminescence
That tells of blind men safe at home.

I lay on my unhealthy back
Warmly snug in my swag
Peering up into the brilliance
While my fire dies at my side
As, drowsily, I digest my dinner.

My black dog, Charlie, is quiet.
He sleeps on, happy with his dreams.
He has no care in the world
After a big feed of nutritious beef,
A soothing benefit to a man and his dog.

As for the longings of a lonely God,
There in the heavens is his handiwork.
And, as a wallaby bounds in the dark,
I marvel at the magnificent Southern Cross
On our nation's flag it is so hot.

The cross, the body of Christ
And its representation in the sky

Is a holy communion of souls,
The bringing together of all mankind
For Jesus to gather into His arms.

But look there, on the left
Is a star, looking bold but small.
It is a watcher noticing Christ's body.
Is he in or out asks Saint Paul?
But I know the joy of being alone.

Dan

Dan, it may surprise
Was loved by everyone
Whose heart was big
And did a jig whenever
He stepped into a room.
His mother was one.
His father was blond.
Tragically they loved
Their oldest son
But now he was gone.
Dan was long gone.
No trace of him was to be found.
He had walked out one night.
He had just up and left
Leaving a life behind
With people who searched,
A police cordon that worked,
For no one was allowed inside.
He had forgotten his pills.
His condition was real
For many to offer derision
But hearts leapt out for Dan.
Maybe he had fallen prey
To a violent man.
Yet, unanimously,
Everyone agreed
Even if it was no reprieve
That he had left on a trek
And was nowhere to be seen.

Picking Day (Mildura)

A westerly rose and fell
Amongst the vine's fat with fruit:
Big grape bunches that hung
Ready for a swift picking
By hands deft and wet,
Slick with the juice that thickened
The tongue with ripened sugar.

Stickily hot and a berry blue,
The inviolate sky is so high
That the farmer can count on
The buckets the pickers had filled
And he was thoroughly content
That his grapes would lend
His rugged fame to his sultanas.

A chant rose in the breeze,
A choir that pierced his heart.
In the shadows of the house,
In the presence of the Almighty,
A salient Hail Mary burst forth
On the wings of hard work
From mouths full of enthusiasm.

A thrilled church had sent to pray,
To build up the picker's mighty ranks,
To catch the excellent harvest
Of the farmer's sanguine efforts,
To see the electrified parish pick
The reverent, white grapes
Deep in his quivering vineyard.

The loyal chant lifted high
As the scorching wind tore aside
Words probing and wise,
A song that soothed muscles
That valiantly smiled in eager eyes,
A prayer acknowledged far and wide
A long way from a church's confines.

Enriched the elements were kind
To ruddy faces full of laughs.
The Hail Mary did lovingly guide
Pickers who had Christ in mind,
And the farmer was to give thanks
As he flung sultanas on to racks
For them to dry in the withering sun.

Prayer

To a haunted, restless spirit
The invasive sword that cuts
Carves an anguish so cruel it stings.
It is agonizing to a defenceless soul
And a divine anchor is needed.

In the inhabited centre of my being
There is solid ground to stand on.
There the essence of the Holy Trinity
Calms the wild and reeling senses
To bring me back to the here and now.

The tender speech of the Lord
Is to divert me from the earth.
The man in there is my guest.
He is a God at His most perfect
Knocking on the door of my lonely heart.

Simple logic has its reward
To tame the violent senses,
Disciplining the urge to rebel,
To bring the flesh under control,
Offering a blessing of my own.

He is a God waiting to be heard.
By the tragedy of man's world
In God's hands joy is to be found.
Affectionately I listen to His still, small voice
Tell me of the enticing fruits of His kingdom.

A distraught society
Offers its many obstacles to prayer

As darts thrown into the backs of escapees
Who flee the dangers of a turbulent sea
Where sharks and monsters prevail.

In prayer, forget the distracting crowd,
Wisely forgo the constant worry,
Listen quietly for God to loudly speak,
Genuinely turn from the outside world
And hear God in heart, mind and soul.

Stolen

"How long have you sat here for?"
The fortunate, old man asked.
"Have you done any work today?"

The youngster shook his head
To stare with a hidden and desolate face
At the tree that swayed just above his head.

With a friendly grin,
The old man leaned towards him.

"Did someone ever tell you?"
He demanded of the young fellow,
"Of the man who did not want to stand
In the shadow of the sun?"

The guilty Avid looked surprised
And, while the breeze tossed a branch
Above his irresolute, hiding place,
The heat of the golden sun
Fell across his pale visage.
But, with an impudent grin
He plucked up his courage
To give the old man a cheeky dig:

"Was he brown?" he asked.
"With skin like leather
Or was he as blind
As a lizard that sits on a desert rock?"

The old man chuckled then sipped his tea,
Hungry to appease the appetite
That he had built up in the orchard that day.

"He was the same as you and me,"
He told the young fellow.
"He had a clean shirt
And he wore a floppy hat.
Expertly he would stand in the heat
To flee from the cold shadow of the sun."

Unwittingly, Avid looked away,
Trying hard to hide his fate
But the old man was not daunted;
Eager, he was quick to follow on.

"All day long
That man chased that hot sun:
A seasoned stayer,
Each time he felt its shadow's cold embrace,
He would shiver and then urge himself on."

The wary, young man thought for awhile
Then he laughed,
"Did he ever capture the sun?" he probed.

"No," the old man replied.
"He got fed up in the heat,
He thought he would chase shadows instead."

Avid began to laugh.
He laughed so hard
That his sides began to ache.

"To this day," the old man continued on,
"That man is hiding from the sun."

Moonlight

Out for a walk last night,
I felt the water splash about my boots;
The rain, sadly, tumble from my raincoat's hood.

I walked beneath bleak lights -
Bright, fluorescent colour that beckons
For me to inspect the crowded and gaily, displayed stalls.

A night to be window shopping, hemmed in by the rain
That makes the lounge resonate, like a prison
Washing the streets that echo to yester years' larrikinism.

A book store with covers and garish colours,
All new and demanding money, a picture of Christ
Dangling from His cross, a testament to man's treachery.

A man with a trombone, in the rain played melancholy
On a street corner with an empty hat nearby -
A lone spectre amongst the couples flowing by, hand in hand.

Wisdom's fortitude lingers in my brain, the constant heart,
The pace that steadies the groping will
That reaches for the need to walk these nostalgic streets.

Patience 1987

I can ignore an itch
No matter how impatient it is
Like a dismal sentry,
A palace guard standing
A silent post rigid;
All of which rebukes
A lust after lunch,
A wavering stance,
An unsubstantiated belief.

"The pain in my feet."

A philosopher's day
Not spent at the front gate,
Letting time pass by,
Is not worth lectatio.
To do as you are asked,
To keep a still stance,
Boring sentry duty is enduring;
It gives me a good mind,
Patience and a smile.

Neil (Died at 47)

Every day the emphatic mosquito
Drove one of my work mates wild.
He always said they were about his bed.
(He died of a heart attack in '75.)

"He was a bit skinny you see."

The anniversary of his death
Is on the odd day when we deliberate,
When we have an hour to recollect,
To angrily fight God's design,
Therefore, it is a time to respect
The desolate effort to comprehend
Why an optimistic man succumbed.

"Together we remember his struggle."

He would admonish the elements
Then tip the water from the bucket;
Not fail to inspect the deserted pot
To look for signs of mosquito larvae.

There is more to the station
Than its flower bed that attracts;
There is the fleeting memory
In the bucket and the vacant pot,
So empty and stacked with rain,
Of a man who died after a short life.
That ended suddenly and without publicity

A New Sunset (The Motor Cycle Accident)

The bed-ridden man grinned.
"Did yah see my fingers?" he asked dramatically.

Tenderly, Leon lifted up his injured hand
Then led it across his body to rest it on his belly,
A patient with a remedy.

"The two small ones," he said gruffly.
He ran a finger over the hidden stumps.
"When I ran into that post I was going too fast,
They were caught between the handle bars
And the wire fence. They were torn right off."

Undaunted, Harry whistled.
Max was the closest to the patient's head
Abruptly, Harry had to push him aside
To have a look at the sad lump himself.

"You poor fellow," he tried his best.
"Did it hurt?" he asked when he was abreast.

The insurgent patient grinned.
"Nah," he joked rebelliously.
Then, incredulously, he added
"I didn't feel a thing,
I don't even remember the crash.
All I can recall is the ride along Railway Ave,
Everything is a complete blank."

Max asked dismally,
"How are you going to work, mate?"
He demanded desperately,
Convinced that Leon was a nonchalant yob.

Delicately, drowsily
The patient shook his head manfully.
Then, with a ginger tenderness
He turned over his torn limb wistfully
To inspect the damage bravely.

"I should be alright," he challenged.
His bravado encouraged
But in fear of his mortality,
His diagnosis did not soften his predicament.

Then, tiredly, he lost interest.
He discharged us, he forgot us.
Sadly, dejected he did not feel like talking
About his new disability, his loss of anatomy.

An Opinion

Adam and Eve were to grieve
They had children as man and woman;
Sons they had who sought God's blessing.

Cain in his garden with a watering can
Like God, so cross, he waters his crops,
His pots, his fertilizers seed the desert lands.

Abel is a shepherd with a staff, a calf.
His pasture is where the grass is wet and lush
The sheep trust him and go where he worships.

When God is favoured there is a race.
A horse in a gallop could not out run
The rivalry between two brothers in a chase.

In an altercation envy is bound to win.
The watering can is heavy and hits.
The herd is left to wander drifting in the wind.

A Lady in a Tower

A Godly spirituality
Is a fleeting prominence
And a lady locked up in a tower
Out of reach, hidden
And brightly garbed in light

Is as close as you can get
To a remarkable, spiritual life
But to stay calm you must
Learn to keep a still mind
And oh, be quiet my beating heart.

In an impenetrable tower,
A lady is as spiritual as you can be.
A soul free of the vile world
Is free of harmful temptation
And, skilfully, there is nothing:

No fleeting disturbance,
No doubtful concerns,
No cares or responsibilities,
No sublime human interaction,
There is just her and her God.

To be that fortunate lady
Would be the luck of all the faithful
But the young, particularly
Have a hardy life to live
And the old sit in a chair and sleep.

Well we might want to be
A monk or an enclosed nun

But life throws up little surprises
To disturb your tranquillity,
To change your winding path.

God tastes your stormy will
And, perhaps, your mettle;
A just God who tests the air
To see which way, you will go
But some say He already knows.

David Rolfe

In vain the police arrived
To help the man who died
Fighting with his walking stick
As his door was kicked in
And his flat screen stolen.

The abhorrent crime happened
In a flash. It was represented
To have occurred in the night
In front of a surprised witness
Not far from his astounded doorstep.

Robert, Joe and Pepper
Had taken his pension
And, as a vulnerable invalid,
David had no other moral support
Other than the amiable love of God.

A friendly ambulance came
Bearing two forthright men
Who were quick to say
That David was stone dead,
That, in the dawn, he had no hope.

Cheap wine was his downfall.
His shocked salty veins were weak
And, to dismay, he had no defence
From the heavy fist that struck,
That knocked him down flat.

His neighbours did not love him.
Truthfully, he was a rogue, a terror,

A damned, horrible felon,
A rebel who deserved his fate
To be bludgeoned late at night.

Gordon, Paul and Genevieve
Said no sorrowful prayer for him.
In truth he was not religious
And never asked for any supplication
So they all believed that he burned in hell.

Strength

In neat rows
His carefully stacked bricks
Stood waiting for the manager to okay;
Nearly a thousand altogether
That he had painstakingly cleaned in the burning rays.

Chipping
Was a thankless and dusty operation.
The contractor received only a few cents
Payment for each re-usable brick that he presented
But, despite the low wage, Jim was still available.

After all, he had a wife,
Bills to pay and, later that day,
A few hours to look forward to in church with his mates.
He had little thought of trying to adapt
To a new and complex workplace.

It was three o'clock.
Running sweat glistened on his eroded cheeks
Mixing thickly with the dust that clung to his red skin.
Chipping with eager swings,
Jim was content.

Bertram

The town as a habit
Had streets as bare of traffic
As tundra is as full of puddles,
Like a puppy playing dead,
Uncertain of any rest.
Yet on Saturday they came,
From east and west -
Farmer's wives with money
To tie up the store's company.

"Love is in the air…"

He played his guitar,
Sang songs of the heart -
A strummer who had stood
On many a town corner.
He was won over by the ladies
Who, every weekend paying,
Would listen to the lilt,
The tilt of his voice
Then drop a ten or a twenty
Into his cowboy's hat.

"As she climbed the stairway to heaven…"

Louise, Heidi and Florence
All revelled in his play,
Glad that in their town
Bertram had chosen to make his way.

The Fifteen-Year-Old Jackaroo

Dust rose in an agitated spiral
In a land desiccated and cracked
By mud flats that sank
Amongst the spinifex tracks.
They were dry and scratched
By the feet of sheep, roos and emus
Captured in a Pilbara paddock.

A sleepy jackaroo on horse back
Dreamily lazed in his saddle
Jostling a tin of Log Cabin
To roll a smoke with one hand
While holding his reins in the other -
A practised echo of the drover
Who hunted sheep in the muster.

A blanket of heat burned
As a thousand flies swarmed
With a flick of the horse's tail,
With a wave of the jackaroo's hand.
As he cursed God for the trouble
But he thought better of it
And he prayed an apologetic Our Father.

Thirst dogged his sore lips
Dry and shackled by the work.
He had no drop of refreshing water
And the hat on his head was no retort
To the sun that warmed the air,
That drove him silently mad
And hampered his search for sheep.

Far into the parched spinifex he rode
And, in contemplation, he closed his eyes,
Passive to the pain in his behind.
Smoothly his saddle was supple
And his horse had a rolling stride
Giving his thoughts a divine edge,
A hope of success in the elements.

Luck was not with him today.
There were no sheep in the paddock.
The other drovers found their mark
But the jackaroo's day was quiet.
He had time to trust in the Lord.
It was a day to find God's favour,
To notice the Almighty in the world.

He had dreams of tumbling hills
That, surprisingly, fell beneath his feet.
He thought of himself as a boy
Who lived in a world of aliens.
This helped him turn to his soul
To find the presence of the Lord
While the land about him was big.

He found his joy in being small
On a day when he had no sheep to manoeuvre.
He had a long moment to drift
While riding a horse in the north-west.
His only company was an ever-present God
Who was a comforting companion
And a buffer between the jackaroo and destruction.

Waylaid

"Look at that tyre!"

The policeman removed his hat
Otherwise he was immaculately garbed -
A town tamer with a harness.
He had a set of blinkers
For any civilian led astray.
The law was his to demand.
It is the public's duty to obey.

"They're a bit bald," he judged.

Johnson was a stranger,
A refugee from another state,
Not that the copper gave a hoot
About his religious fate.
He was mad about the car.
It was on his slate
That Johnson clean it up soon
Or its four cylinders
Would be led to their doom.

"I have two new ones," Johnson told him.

He led the copper to the boot
Where he kept his gear.
In there was his tucker
Kept safe was his swag.
Nestled between them, in disdain,
Awash in the smell of rubber,
Were two, new, six-inch tyres.

"Good," the policeman smiled.

A Hill Climb

Parked on a verge,
The wheels are turned
On a hill that is divine.
At the top is a light.
The bottom is a crash,
Dented and trashed.
The instructor is a man,
Calm and assured
While she is demure,
Legs that are twigs,
Arms that are sticks,
A prayer she can say -
Jesus, Mary and Joseph she asks.

'If she will survive the hill climb?"

She must turn the key,
Release the hand brake,
Ease up on the clutch,
Try not to say much,
Wonder about lunch,
Do as the instructor ask,
Press the accelerator hard,
Climb the hill to the top
To reach the cup of success.
Then smile and look impressed
As a cheeky and lucky penitent
Her skinny fingers could operate
A huge car with her new licence.

A Wage 1994

Eager for a decent pay,
Mark and James have their caps in hand.
Together they beat at their breasts
As they work, in the heat, to impress
Axel, the farmer, in the Barossa Valley.

A blue Ferguson roared into life
Ready for Mark to gather the produce:
The buckets of red, shiny grapes,
Ripe with the farmer's wine, Shiraz
That Mark stacked onto the trailer.

James drove the ancient tractor.
He is as honest as TV's MacGyver.
On the job he is an experienced man,
A hand who knows his way about
A dazzling vineyard and its juicy crop.

For a steady ten dollars an hour
Both are eager to work their guts out,
Preparing the succulent grapes
For fermentation, for conversion
At the old and local, smelly winery.

Every week Axel, the farmer, was quick.
Wisely he was certain to penny pinch.
He said that there was no overtime,
That the work on the farm was casual
So, the essential Mark and James knew their lot.

Both men were on their toes
But they were anticipating the work

And for six weeks they bent their backs
To pick up the buckets of full, lush berries
While they enjoyed the sun's warmth.

The two workers also made friends
Of dear old Daisy, Dozy and Megs
Who picked the wine grapes -
Big, red bunches that they tasted
While they were paid by the bucket at one dollar each.

The Newsagent

With the early, morning sun
Blasting, sparkling, glowing
Awakening an inquisitive Ezra,
A private but lonely, old man,
A widower with a short, white beard
Who was still in tender mourning.
And his traumatic days were restless
As he remembered a companion,
The lingering joy of an abundant Edwina
Who offered an amorous response
To his softly, spoken words
While he cooked breakfast.

He drank his Lipton tea
And ate his fill of bacon and eggs.
His heart gladdened by the routine
Then, with trepidation in his soul
He opened his famous shop -
A proud premises that was alive
With colour and interest:
A busy newsagent, a life
On the hectic, main street
That split a small, country town.

On the dot at seven o'clock
There was a slight chill
And in his mind Ezra was disarmed.
His long days were mired
But his isolated spirits were uplifted
With the arrival of a patron,
A jaded and tired truck driver
Named Comanche Johnny

Who bought the daily newspaper
And played a thrilling Lotto.

Then, to cause a mild consternation,
The divine Jenni came for writing paper.
A robust storm in a tea cup,
She was unruffled by his stern gaze
As she paid in cash, in a flash
She was young and flirtatious,
A jewel in Christ's crown.
She was a devout acquaintance.

Ezra's ever, hopeful soul believed
He read the good book avidly
And he calmly did his sums.
Confidently he was a just man,
A steady and voracious penitent
And, to all, he was no listless bum.

With angry, bitter words
His much-loved children had left.
Two bouncing boys and a girl,
Jeremiah, Isaiah and Ruth.
Long gone was a family
That had drifted apart,
None of them attuned to God's will.

A faithful Ezra missed them all
But an elegant Christ was in his soul
And he listened to His word
By reading the Gospel,
Taking the time to peruse
The books of Wisdom.
The most familiar

Was the book of Job
For Job had lost his family
To the pleasures of the world.

Ezra rested his heavy spirit
In the praise of the indomitable Christ
In the presence of his smiling customers
Who had no idea of his thoughts
That he was considering, in prayer,
The day when he would turn
To an everlasting Lord, his saviour
Where he would see his wife
And be alone no more.

Picking Apples in Orange

"Hello, Rory." "Hi yah, Clarissa."

She was the first to clamber in;
A scrawny girl with long, brown hair
That hung in dusty streaks
With a hint of despair
About the haggard cheeks of her face.

"Did you pick many bins?"
Rory asked inquisitively.

"We managed seven or eight,"
She was heard to say victoriously.

Theo climbed in to sit beside her.
He was quick to give Rory a smile
To thank him for the lift.
His hair was curly and,
Like his eyes, brown and shiny,
Glistening like two wet pebbles in his olive face.
In his jeans and ragged shirt
He was a man who looked comfy;
A notoriously, hard, headed bohemian
And to distress his beard made him look skint.

Harry leaned over his seat,
To offer them an apple each.

On the Bus

It was on the 755
That, incredibly, it was determined thus
That a baby had begun to protest.
A stranger was the first to react:
His grey hair nodding,
His wrinkled face brilliant
As he gave an ecstatic smile.

"Who is a beautiful, baby girl?"

The mother was young,
A blond, blue, eyed bounty
Who talked with God, as a mate,
A conversation that never ends,
She did not turn her head,
Made no effort to stop
The old man's glee -
Her baby's big, eyed ploy
To remain entranced
By the turn of events,
The smile that lit up his space
On their journey into the west.

"Who is having a good time, then?"

His stop materialized.
Reluctantly he shuffled off
To reminisce on the I.D.
On a community that bridged
On the elation of the young and old
Who made a home for a family on stage.

The Music

A committed poet,
A singer without glamour,
Mike was a hip-hop artist
Who generously announced
That we should praise God
With a zealous start.
Mike had an enthusiastic stride
But to his stone, deaf mates
His huge, musical aspirations
Were all religious gobbledy-gook
And he lived alone with his Lord.

The open door of the Holy Spirit
Filled his contemplative soul
And he surrendered to the light
With the wise words of a penitent:

"In the shadows do not hide
Lost and without courage
When you can shine
As a big-hearted Christian."

A mystic who had sense
Who called men to the music
Not to mystify, not to muddle
But to open the mind to the Lord,
Offering to the heart, to the soul
A mystery that can be grasped
By the poor, the sorrowful
And the downtrodden.

The Break Up

"Please don't go!"

Pam had a winsome child
And locked in her angelic arms
Her boy was thankfully silent.
Inaudibly, he suckled on his pacifier
And watched with wide, open eyes
While his innocent gaze mirrored
The pit of rejection in her own spirit.

"I've had enough!" Karl shouted,
"Of the baby and you.
I have a life to live
With drugs in my bag
To sell to the decadent
On the streets made of gold!"

With that he was gone.
The boy's terrifying father had left.
No trace of him was to be found
In Pam's empty heart
Or in her irate home.

She was soundly guarded by her girlfriends
Who gravely helped her to forget
That her days were filled with sadness.

With compassion they said:
"Pam, you should read this."

It was a book of constructive prayer
And a new bible held in one hand

Which she took and looked through
Uncertain of what it was she perused
But wisely it was easy to discern
That a patient Christ was the culprit
As an optimistic God who sought to comfort.

Opportunity knocks
And in the restful words of a prayer
A mother's dear heart was drawn
To listen to the eternal voice
Searching for the God within.
The thirsty possibility was there
And her mind lost its terrible distress
As she gently reached for her soul
To praise with affection her peaceful Lord.

A Referendum

Part I

Spreadeagled perfectly
Like a sky-diver cogitating,
The troubled Ben Clifton slept fitfully
As Sydney passed so stridently
Below his patch work window sill -
A work of domestic bliss.

He drifted in and out
Of his furtive and heavenly visitation.
A man without ambition,
Happy to be a labourer
In a realm without contemplation,
A land that causes consternation.

Clearly the agitated voices
Of the developing world
Echoed in his quarters
And, rebelliously, the victim's dreams
Began to dislocate symbolically.
He was alone with his nightmares.

In one corner of his room
A colour television spluttered
With the rhythmic sounds
Of an advert's skulduggery;
An impersonal, forgetful itinerary
That was unpardonable in its ferocity.

So, the dish ran away with the spoon,
Ben Clifton's porridge was cold.

A sturdy train driver,
He had worked the night shift
And, without eating his breakfast,
He was quick to fall asleep.

Part II

With a stern disposition,
A distant woman rigidly intoned
With the awakening words
That hammered into his mind
The midday news bulletin
Rashly filled with a cast of felons,

Unaware that she was creating
A small disharmony,
A hopeless descent,
In the enclosed serenity
Of the railway man's environment.
Her punctuality was just perfect.

The anchor's words ushered in
The disdained celebrity
Of Australia's top politicians
Who proudly displayed their panache
To a rampant, hungry journalism
Who wrote of a hopeful population.

Labor men in red ties speculated
On a vile government's stance
With a diligence that influenced
Their ability to collectively
Wow a perplexed country
To alarm a robust community

Their incisive voices
Informed an allied nation

That the opposition had devised
An Australian flag, a pennant – one that
Proudly displayed the Southern Cross
On a sky-blue background.

Part III

In its top left-hand corner,
The national emblem
Had proudly found a place -
An emu and its stern resemblance,
A healthy, hopeful reconciliation
For a dismayed nation.

The emaciated features
Of that poet Henry Lawson,
Who said his best mate was a yid,
Was in the flag's top right-hand corner,
Who dwarfed the tiny echidna pictured beneath him -
An icon that was ready to defend its position

Majestically robed,
In the bottom left-hand corner
The image of Dame Nellie Melba
Faithfully sung of a woman's enthusiasm -
Her flamboyance, her acceptance,
Of her country's division.

The captivating notes
Of Waltzing Matilda
Boldly claimed the turbulence,
Threatening to bring the startled Ben Clifton
Out of his distracted entreaty
And strictly onto his feet,

Where he would have tilted,
Abysmally unshaven, enraptured,

And rigidly in a defiant salute
That is usually reserved
For the king and his officers -
A demonstration of his rebellion.

Part IV

With a wrathful tone,
The news program came to a halt.
Acrimoniously, once more,
In shameful wrapping, the adverts
Were replayed by the intrusive piracy.
Keeping an insane society bored,

And, resentfully, dolefully,
The room's only visible life form,
Fiercely recaptured his scattered senses
And, demoralized, he was able to identify
With a hurt and incredulous disbelief
The origin of the electronic gunnery.

With a blunt exclamation,
Ben Clifton's wisdom howled.
At midday he fought to stay calm.
Timidly, in a fight to take control,
He opened his weary, blue eyes
To observe that the sun was up.

Keen to stare at a large DTV,
With a deep recrimination
Recalling his night of labour,
How, afterwards, he had fallen asleep
With the tawdry distraction still on,
That spoke to a blockaded man.

An anchor had introduced
A referendum that embattled

The fierce republicans
And a displaced royalty
On a day that was unforgiving -
A democratic day of decision

www.ingramcontent.com/pod-product-compliance
Lightning Source LLC
Chambersburg PA
CBHW030202100526
44592CB00009B/404